BWR

MANAGE YOUR MONEY LIKE THE 1%

A STEP BY STEP GUIDE TO MANAGING YOUR MONEY

D1496409

XSCaPE
PUBLISHING
xscapepublishing.com

Our Company

In 2019, Adrian Kennedy began publishing books for independent authors from his office in Charlotte, North Carolina. His goal was to provide authors with more options and control over the publishing process at prices anyone could afford.

Today, the family owned and operated, Xscape Publishing company still continues to honor the founder's tradition of providing high-quality products and valuable services to the community.

TABLE OF CONTENTS

ABOUT THE AUTHORS

KELLY RHODES

Hello, everyone, I'm Kelly Rhodes, I'm from Fort Worth, Texas. I grew up going to private school all my life until middle school when I moved to Burleson Texas. In high school, I played sports specifically Football where I think I started my ridiculous work ethic. I'm a very competitive person so I genuinely feel I'm always the hardest working person in whatever I do. After graduating high school I went to Louisiana Tech due to their quarter system. This is where really my interesting journey begins. During my first year of college, I was an engineering major and hated it. I almost flunked out my first quarter finishing with a 2.1 GPA. At that point I knew engineering was not the major for me. I ended up changing my major to business management after my first quarter. After my 2nd quarter at tech I had to leave school for a quarter due to financial issues. I came back during the summer session and never looked back. Despite not selecting the right major and sitting out a quarter, I still was able to graduate with a business management degree in three years. After graduation, I moved to West Texas where I am currently working in the oil field as a safety professional. I became part of BWR back in January of 2019 and it has been a wild and amazing ride. I wanted to get involved because I knew that the black community consistently has been overlooked when providing information about wealth. So I wanted to create a platform that shows people that there are people out there that look like us doing amazing things financially. Not only did I want to highlight those people I also wanted people to learn thousands of ways in which they could take action to build generational wealth. I have also begun my investment investing journey in 2019 becoming a silent investor and I am curious to see what the future holds.

JARED SPILLER

What's good y'all it's Jared. I was born in Richardson, Texas and moved to Ruston, Louisiana when I was young. I grew up in Ruston and attended Louisiana Tech University which was where I met David and Kelly and eventually would end up leading me to meet Jalen through my fraternity. I came across the book Rich Dad Poor Dad from a fraternity brother of mine (S/O Henry). And, after reading the book I was hooked on financial education. I always had an interest in money and my roommates and I were notorious for our money-making schemes. But, after reading RDPD our mindsets changed forever. Fast forward one year later and while talking about our business plans and lack of support David and I start Black Wealth Renaissance as a passion project to raise awareness about financial literacy. Fast forward another year and we've built a huge community dedicated to the education of our people. We've grown so much and continue to grow and I'm so happy about that because to me it means that we are reaching more people and hopefully helping more people, which was why we started. Personally, I use different micro-investing methods as of now while increasing my income to purchase my first property or househack. I'm currently going into my first tax season as a preparer and I'm studying for my notary exam in June. I hope that you find this book to be helpful and insightful and if you need anything else feel free to reach out you know where to find Black Wealth Renaissance!

DAVID BELLARD

What's up fam, my name is David Fitzgerald Bellard, Jr. I was born on December 7, 1994, in the rural town of Opelousas, LA. From a young age, I have always shown a high aptitude for learning and an understanding of the value of hard work. I was "the smart kid". The one that everyone votes as Most Likely To Succeed. You know, the kid everyone expected to be a doctor, lawyer, engineer, or something like that.

Like many people, I thought that this would be my path, so I worked hard and earned an academic scholarship along with a chance to play football at Louisiana Tech University. Against the advice of just about everyone at the university, I decided to major in engineering & quickly found myself overwhelmed by my workload as a student-athlete. This challenged me to try harder, but I ultimately concluded that engineering wasn't for me and ended up changing my major to Biology during my sophomore year.

My major pivot was not well planned and was done with the intention of keeping me on track to graduate in 4 years. Shortly after changing my major, I made the decision to leave football and get a job. This provided me with income and an improvement in my grades but I still had an issue. I did not have a real plan. During my junior year, I realized that I would much rather do business & marketing, but I wasn't trying to get a bunch of student loan debt. So during the summers, Jared, Kelly & I began to work on various side ventures trying everything from dropshipping to forex to making an influencer page. We didn't know it at the time, but those summers began to sow the seeds of what would grow to be BWR.

After graduating, I started the process of becoming an EMT and during that time I was introduced to Rich Dad Poor Dad by one of my best friends/co-founders Jared Spiller. The book opened my eyes to the realm of financial literacy and ignited my passion for entrepreneurship. From that point forward I felt that it was imperative to share this information with people who look like me based on a firm belief that a large part of our issues is rooted in economics. If we knew this type of information earlier we would see many of the changes we wish to see in the black community as well as a higher level of achievement. That is exactly what we aim to accomplish with this platform; educating the black masses on the importance of financial literacy & group economics by providing them with examples as well as the tools and resources to help them attain wealth.

JALEN CLARK

Hello I'm Jalen Clark a 25-year-old entrepreneur from the small town of Opelousas, Louisiana. Growing up in a small town I always knew there was more to life and was determined to uncover those secrets. I grew up the oldest of 5 in a single-parent household. Life wasn't easy for us with my mother providing for 5 children and herself. I had to grow up quickly and be an example for my younger siblings. I graduated College from

Northwestern State University In Natchitoches Louisiana with a bachelor's degree in business administration concentrated in marketing. Upon graduating from College I quickly realize the corporate life was not a place for me since I'm constantly challenging the rules and thinking of ways to innovate. I felt limited and unchallenged in some positions. I have tried many hands at entrepreneurship and learned plenty of lessons through those ventures. I joined BWR In February of 2019 through one of my best friends David Bellard. My main reasoning for joining Black Wealth Renaissance is to make a difference in someone's life who could benefit from the tools and resources our platform was providing. I know the black community is severely underserved and highly overlooked when it comes to resources, education, and opportunities, so we Took on the responsibility of proving those necessities. We do this by providing courses and resources to educate oneself.

We also highlight successful African-American entrepreneurs and business professionals. Providing examples and role models for the youth and their parents is pivotal in changing the narrative. I look to spread the message of financial literacy to anyone who is willing to learn. I'm beyond blessed to be on this team and can't wait to see the impact we have on others.

MANAGE YOUR MONEY LIKE THE 1%

INTRODUCTION

To be considered a part of the 1% in America, you must have an annual income of $421,000. However, that number may seem very overwhelming and impossible to reach when you look at your current situation. But you need to understand that this book is not about how to make $421,000, it is about how to manage your money like you are making $421,000. This is not saying that you cannot implement the steps we teach in this book to make $421,000 annually, because we believe with hard work and dedication you can.

An article written by CNBC in January of 2019 stated that 60% of Americans would go into debt if they ran into a $1,000 emergency. For the percentage to be that high is absolutely unacceptable, and Black Wealth Renaissance feels it is our responsibility to educate the masses on how to manage their money. Financial education is not emphasized in the school system, and many parents do not understand financial literacy, continuing the struggle of living paycheck to paycheck.

Here at Black Wealth Renaissance, we want you to understand the principles of building wealth so that you can create generational wealth. We are going to show you step by step. How to manage your money like the 1%, and if you do these steps consistently long term, it will allow you to grow your wealth exponentially. If you don't get anything else out of this book, the most important thing to remember is what I'm about to tell you. If you want to become a part of the 1%, you have to start changing your mindset about money and seeing money as a tool!

STEP 1: Stop the Bleeding

So, let's start by understanding how the 1% gain and, most importantly, maintain their wealth. The 1% understands the flow of their money and how to allocate it. So, the first step is something we here at Black Wealth Renaissance-like to call "stopping the bleeding."

Before we begin, ask yourself this; do I really know where every dollar from my income is going?

If you can't answer this with an exact mapping of your money, then there is still some bleeding going on with your finances, and this ebook will give you the necessary tools to control it. To better understand what we mean, let's dive into stopping your financial bleeding.

So say you accidentally cut or hurt yourself, the first thing that David, as a former emergency responder, and Kelly, as a safety coordinator, are trained to do is to stop the bleeding. No matter how bad the injury may be, you must first stop the bleeding then assess the damage after the bleeding is under control. Now we know you didn't get this ebook to learn about first aid, so how does this method apply to your finances? You may ask.

When you are first starting, you want to assess what damage you are doing to your finances. There are many ways to do this, so let's look at a couple. First, let's start with the old school way, where you can take out a piece of paper, draw a line down the middle of it. Write down and add up all your monthly expenses on one side of the paper, such as rent, mortgage, food, bills, car payment, gas, and any other monthly expenses you may have.

Next, you want to add up all your income for the month; write that down on the other side of the paper, including any side hustles that you may have but are not linked to a business account. Once you have totaled both sides, you can see where your money is going every month. Another way to do this is through apps. Multiple apps will track your spending, one that we use is called Truebill. Truebill can be linked to your bank accounts, and it will track your income, expenses and give you monthly reports automatically. But for this information to be accurate, you must only use debit cards that are linked to your Truebill account. It is still an excellent way for you to track where your money is going.

After you have completed this; it is time to start asking yourself, do I really need that? Do I really need to eat out every day? Can I afford that $600 car payment? Do I need to get those $200 Jordan's, or that $100 purse? These are hard questions you must ask yourself to be like the 1%. The 1% may have nice cars, clothes, jewelry, and houses now, but when they were starting, they did not spend that type of money! They understood the concept of affordability. So the best question to ask yourself is, what can I afford? (A good rule of thumb to remember is if you can not purchase it twice, you can not afford it.)

STEP 2: Dress Your Wounds

Budgeting is telling your money where to go before you receive it. It's as simple as that; you have to tell every dollar where to go and how to work so that it won't be working against you. At Black Wealth Renaissance, we like to look at ourselves as a business. With that in mind, look at your income as employees, if you allow your employees to sit there without being told what their job is, you will start paying them to do nothing, and hence, to your disadvantage.

After completing step one, you have done the bulk of the work when it comes to budgeting. Now you must analyze your personal finances to create your **personal budget**[23]. First, you need to assign your money to your necessities, such as housing (including housing bills), food, and transportation. Calculate the cost of this monthly and subtract it from your income.

Your necessities have now been accounted for, so let's look at your debt, which may consist of credit cards, student loans, personal loan(s), or even car payment. We will go into greater detail later, but for now, start by paying the minimum payment as you get your budget together. Add all the debt payments up for the month and subtract it from your income.

Next are your miscellaneous expenses such as shopping, Netflix, alcohol, Spotify or Apple Music, etc. Looking at these expenses, can you see anything you can do without? Maybe that cable bill? Or going out every weekend? These are expenses that most people can cut out, and by doing so, will allow you to create extra cash flow[10] every month. You don't always have to do completely without, but you can cut down on certain things. Maybe instead of eating out 4 times a week, you can cut it down to 2 or 3. Little adjustments like this to your lifestyle will allow you to create extra cash flow to pursue your goals.

Once you have added up the miscellaneous expenses for the month and subtracting it from your income, it is time to see the cash flow. Is your cash flow positive or negative? Congrats to you if you are in the positive as you are on your way to managing your money like the 1%. No need to feel stressed if your cash flow is negative, but take a deep breath to concentrate on how we can change our financials into a positive cashflow. You should try to subtract expenses in reverse order of our process, which means, taking out any expenses that you can survive without, miscellaneous expenses, and debt. You should never go into necessities as that is the basics you need to maintain life.

As we have talked about how to cut down on miscellaneous expenses, let's discuss how to alter your debt. To change your **liability**[21], you can defer or switch to an income-based payment for student loans. You can also refinance your car or mortgage to allow cheaper payments per month. Take note that refinances are subject to approval from the bank. The goal is to have positive **cash flow**, so sometimes you must make sacrifices to accomplish your financial goals.

Just by doing this step, you are going to be ahead of most people. Most people don't budget because it seems too hard, or it's too much math. We've even come across people that believe their low income will not allow them to budget. This is simply false; many people become overwhelmed or just don't know where to start when it comes to budgeting. This is the beginning step in building your financial foundation; once you can complete step one, the rest of the steps become so much easier. **BWR HAS MADE IT EASY FOR YOU TO START BUDGETING WITH A BUDGETING TEMPLATE DOWNLOAD IT NOW!!!**

GET THE BWR FREE BUDGET TEMPLATE HERE!
https://bit.ly/2Tr3JtM

BWR BUDGET TEMPLATE WALKTHROUGH VIDEO
https://bit.ly/2Toe4Xq

STEP 3: Prepare For The Worst

The next step is to create an **emergency fund**[14]. Wealthy people maintain an emergency fund of at least 3-6 months' worth of expenses. This step is vital because everyone goes through life and life happens to everyone. You never know when your car will break down, or when you may become very ill, so it's just better to be financially ready for it. Saving 3-6 months of expenses may seem like a daunting task, but we will walk you through it.

First, after you have a positive cash flow, you want to save that cashflow to have at least one month of total expenses. That's the first goal; once you have completed the first goal, the next is to save at least 3 months of your overall expenses. Next is the final goal of 6 months' worth of total expenses. You want to do it in these steps and only focus on one goal at a time because 6 months' worth of total expenses can seem like a ton of money to save. But tackling each set goal one at a time will allow you to not feel overwhelmed.

The emergency fund is not for you to spend on vacation or going out, it is **ONLY** for emergencies. The emergency fund is essential because when life does happen, you might not have planned for it, but you will be financially ready. You will have great peace of mind once you have built your emergency fund.

BWR TIP: High-Interest Savings Account

Here are some tips on where to put your money when saving and how to stick to your budget. Let's talk about where to put your emergency fund. When you are dealing with a large sum of money like your emergency fund, you don't want to keep it in cash. So, don't put that money under your mattress, in a shoebox, in your closet, or bury it. Since this money is not going to be invested you want to keep this money in a high-interest savings account.

High-interest savings accounts are basically savings accounts that pay you better than normal. The average **interest rates**[19] for a savings account is .09%, which means you will only earn $0.09 per $100 you keep in that account. To earn $1, you would have to have over $1,100 in the account. That's not worth it, so we recommend a high-interest savings account, which on average have an interest rate between 2.1%-2.5%. So, let's look at those examples again; if you were to keep $100 in a 2.5% interest savings account, you would earn $2.50. That may not seem like a lot, but it's a better rate of return than a regular savings account, and you are making money on your money without investing. Here are some banks that offer these high-interest savings account; Ally, Wealthfront, and Synchrony. Remember this money is only for emergencies so try not to access this money for anything other than that.

Want to know how Kelly saved up 8 months' worth of expenses and $12,000 for an investment? Here's the step by step guide and how you can implement this strategy too. To begin, you must have a bank account and an employer who allows direct deposit with multiple accounts. He first set up 3 checking accounts, one for each expense category (Necessities, Debt, Miscellaneous), and 1 saving account for his emergency fund. He then calculated, on average, how much each expense was per paycheck and deposited that money into each specific checking account. Whatever was leftover was deposited into his savings account. He then added automatic payments for his expenses linked to each expense account. This allowed him to create an automatic budget, so he could take the stress out of distributing his paycheck each time. Using this method will enable you to put your budget on autopilot. Money can become stressful; this is just one way to relieve the stress from your life.

STEP 4: Welcome To Rehab

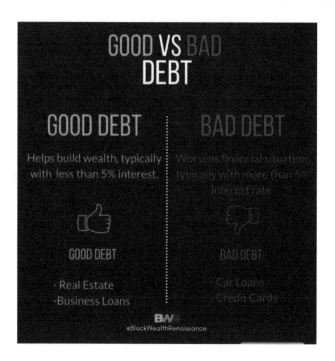

Step 4, after saving for your emergency fund, next is to pay off debt. First, you must understand the difference between good vs. **bad debt**[7]. **Good debt**[16] is debt that helps you leverage to build wealth. Real estate deals & business loans are great examples of leveraging the bank's money to help you build wealth. We will go more on how to invest in real estate later in the book. Bad debt typically has interest rates higher than 5%. Car loans and credit cards are examples of bad debts that have high-interest rates. These types of debts are what you need to focus on when it comes to paying off debt.

Debt consolidation[11] is a way to refinance your loan with extended repayment terms. Meaning instead of having loans of $5,000 at 15%, $5,000 at 11%, $5,000 at 12%, you may be able to take a loan for $15,000 at an interest rate of 13%. There are two common ways to consolidate debt, **balance transfers**[8], and personal loans. The example above is how to consolidate debt with a personal loan. Balance transfers are a way for you to move credit card debt from one credit card to the other, a lot of times you can do this with 0% interest for a certain amount of time. For example, Chase Bank may have a promotional offer on a particular credit card for 12 months and 0% interest on balance transfers. So let's say you have $4,000 worth of credit card debt at a 19% interest rate you may be able to do a balance transfer, to transfer the $4,000 balance to a new card at a 0% interest rate for 12 months. These two ways will allow you to pay less interest when paying down your debts, ultimately putting money back in your pockets.

There are two strategies when it comes to paying off debts. Strategy #1 is called the **avalanche method**[6]; this is the method that is going to leave you with the most money possible back in your bank account. This strategy consists of paying off the highest interest rate first, then once that is paid off, go to the next highest interest rate on a continuous process. By strategizing on the highest interest rate debt first, financially speaking, it's going to save you the most money in the long run. For example, if you have 3 different credit card debts with **APRs**[5] of 25%, 19%, and 17% it would make the most sense to pay off the card with the 25% interest rate first because that is the money you are being charged the most for borrowing. After paying off the highest interest account, you would then take the same amount you paid for that card and apply it to the next highest interest account, saving you even more money by paying off that debt faster than the first.

The second method of paying off debts is the approach popularized by Dave Ramsey, which is called the **snowball method**[30]. For this method you will be paying off the smallest debt balance you have first. This allows you to get the small debt taken care of, and freeing up cash flow to put towards the next lowest debt balance. Many advocate this method because it can create a psychological boost that you see results, which may keep you on track. The downside is that you may end up paying more interest, depending on your debt. Once you have mastered the art of getting out of debt, it will allow you to focus on planning for the future.

STEP 5: Doctor's Orders

Step 5, after creating an avalanche or snowball effect on your debt, you should look at retirement accounts. The first one you should consider if you can get it is an employer match retirement account. You should take advantage of any sponsored retirement plan matching. If your employer offers **401K**[1] matching, you should always take it. Many employers offer a 401K match where they match dollar for dollar up to a certain point of how much you contribute to your 401K account. For example, if you contribute $1,500 into your 401K, your employer will match and put in an additional $1,500 into your 401K. This is what many people call free money.

Many investments will not give you a 100% risk-free guaranteed return, such as a 401K employer match. Not every employer will offer this so do your **due diligence**[13] and see if your employer does. So go in and ask your employer if they offer an employer match on a 401K. If they do find out how much they offer and contribute the max, but you need to get the employer match. Everyone wants free money, why not take advantage of it?

The other retirement account you should invest in, especially if your employer doesn't offer 401K, is a **Roth IRA**[26]. This is an account that allows you to invest after-tax dollars into it, where the money you make inside the account is completely tax-free by the time you are 59 ½. This allows you to get decades of growth and compound interest that works in your favor completely tax-free. When trying to grow your wealth, this step is monumental because it allows you to plan for the future & have access to these accounts for leverage.

BWR TIP: Roth vs. Traditional

There are two different types of **IRA's**[18] & 401K's, Roth & traditional. To keep it simple Roth IRA's & 401K's use after-tax dollars which means that you will get taxed at your current tax rate and all growth earned in the account is tax-free. Whereas in traditional IRA's & 401K's use pre-tax dollars in the retirement account. Using pre-tax dollars means all contributions will not be taxed until you decide to take the money out of the account. You will be taxed at that future tax rate including the growth earned in the account. With traditional retirement accounts, all contributions are tax-deductible each year. So if you contribute $5,000 to your traditional 401K you can deduct $5,000 from your taxes. It may be extremely beneficial for you to conduct a consultation with a tax professional or financial advisor before deciding which retirement account is best for you.

STEP 6: Apply Pressure

The next step is for you to use any money you have leftover from your budget to invest in yourself so that you can begin to make more money. Now you may ask, well, what does it actually mean to invest in yourself? Investing in yourself is putting your money, time, and effort into ventures that will benefit you in the future. There is a multitude of ways to invest in yourself; you could read books, learn a new skill, take a course, pay for coaching, etc. **Self-education**[28] & action at this step is pivotal. You are going to reach a point where you will feel like you have done as much as you can to save, and you are going to want to make more money. You can only save so much money before you hit that wall that you can't get past until you increase your income. You may have to look at switching jobs, changing businesses, or starting a new side hustle. To many, this would be difficult. However, because you have an emergency fund and you are paying off a debt, you can take a little more risk to begin to try to make more money. Whatever it may be, this is the point where you increase your income and get to the point where you can manage your money like the 1%.

After you have completed each step, you should start investing in **taxable accounts**[32] or make any other investments. This is after you have: budgeted, created an emergency fund, paid off debt, funded retirement accounts, and invested in yourself, then, you are now ready for the final step. Investing in these taxable accounts may mean opening up a **brokerage account**[9] to start trading **stocks**[31], or begin investing in real estate or creating your own business. This step is all about creating passive income & increasing your income streams. This allows you to have more money to save & reinvest back into this step.

Now it's time to decide how much risk you are willing to take in your effort to make extra cash. It all depends on you and your current financial position. Before you begin this leg of your marathon, you will need some serious self-evaluation. You need to start asking yourself questions like;

What would I like to invest in that I could turn a profit?

What can I invest in that I already understand?

What is my risk tolerance? (Aka how much are you willing to lose)

And how can I mitigate some of those risks?

How quickly am I realistically expecting,
wanting results and what do the results look like?

These questions will be integral to figuring out where to start your personal journey and how to benchmark your progress as you go. This is so important because many people's patience doesn't align with their pockets. It is very hard (not impossible) to turn $500 into $50,000, but how you do it depends on your plan. Two quick examples right:

Jared is more impatient and wants to achieve financial independence rather quickly (let's say 2-5 years) and has a lower income but more free time in his schedule, considering he works 9-5 Monday through Friday but hates his job and wants to leave. Let's say Kelly is more patient with the growth of his money, earns more than Jared, and actually loves his job but looking for extra income.

Obviously, Jared is going to want to flip his money faster, considering that he hates his job. In this instance, everything that works for Kelly, who earns more and loves his job, may not work for Jared because their situations are different. So Kelly may be fine investing in 20 shares of Apple in 1980 when they had their first IPO[20] at $22 per share and waiting until present-day 2019, where Apple stocks currently valued at around $260 per **share**[29]. After spending approximately 440 dollars initially, he would stand to gain $5200 by cashing in all his stock and would profit $4800 overall after the initial cost of the stock. For someone that enjoys their job and happily enjoying the **appreciation**[3] of their stock and **dividends**[12], or someone who isn't in a rush, this plan can work!

For Jared, who hates his job and has less money, he is probably going to have to take a few more chances with his money than Kelly to achieve the same results because he has less disposable income to invest and also trying to achieve freedom quicker. Assuming he doesn't want to hate his job for 40 years while his stock grows. Instead of the traditional buy and hold stock investing, he may be more inclined to invest in himself to learn how to trade **stock options**[32] and access LEVERAGE to grow his money exponentially.

We are to explain that neither of these methods is wrong. They both just require an extreme amount of honesty with yourself to decide where you are and what you can do with what you have. Our goal is to help you understand your **risk tolerance**[24] so that you can better map out your journey to financial independence.

Furthermore, neither of those methods are incorrect because managing your money like the 1%, for the most part, is prepared to take a risk. You're putting money away in an emergency fund and paying down the debt, so that if you start a business or make an investment and lose money, it won't be devastating to your personal finances. The goal is to be able to invest without worrying about losing everything you already have.

So now that you are starting to assess your situation and risk tolerance, you're probably wondering, "what are my options," and we're glad you asked! The rest of this chapter will be dedicated to explaining that.

UNDERSTANDING YOUR RISK TOLERANCE

BWR
eBlackWealthRenaissance

How comfortable you are with the ups and downs of investing is called your risk tolerance.
Take a quiz and start discovering your own risk tolerance at https://njaes.rutgers.edu/money/assessment-tools/

All investments involve some degree of risk. To make informed investment decisions, you should identify those risks and gauge your willingness to accept them.

Match your risk tolerance

Tolerance Level	Low $	Medium $ $	High $ $ $
Investor's Behavior	Loses sleep whenever investments decline in value.	Doesn't fret over small declines, but stresses about bigger ones.	Not bothered by ups and downs, just wants to maximize returns over the long term.
Investments to Consider	Basic savings account Money Market Deposit Account (MMDA) Certificates of Deposit	Stocks of large, established, financially healthy companies Mutual funds that balance stock and bond holdings	Sophisticated, higher-risk investments Stocks of startup companies

Adjust investments as risk tolerance changes

Your risk tolerance will change as your investment goals, financial situation and life experience change.

Generally, the longer the length of time until you need your money, the more risk you can afford to take.

Risk tolerance is highest for investments you've chosen to meet far away goals, such as retirement, because your investments have more time to potentially recover from drops in value.

Risk tolerance is lowest for investments to meet short-term goals, such as saving up for education cost, vacations and other instances when you will need the money sooner.

LOW-RISK INVESTMENTS

CD'S

When we talk about CD's we are not talking about the disc you put in your car stereo, we are discussing certificates of deposits. This is a federally insured savings account that offers you fixed interest rates and a fixed date of withdrawal, aka **maturity date**[22]. So what is the difference between a traditional savings account and a CD, you may ask? With CD's you have what's called a maturity date, which is the date that you are allowed to take out the money invested without any penalty. Meaning that you can't withdraw any money from the CD without penalties until that specific date. With traditional savings accounts, you can take & put money in relatively freely. CD's offer different maturity dates, as short as a few days, up to decades. The reason for the longer length is that it restricts you from using that money for an extended period, which the bank will offer a higher interest rate, and the opposite is exact for shorter maturity date CDs. Some of the best CD interest rates range from 2% to 3%, depending on the length of the maturity date. Meaning if you invest $3,000 into 2.5% at the maturity date of 5 years, you will earn $399.43 in interest over that 5 years. CD's is a good way to leave money that you do not plan to use at any time soon to gain some interest.

BONDS

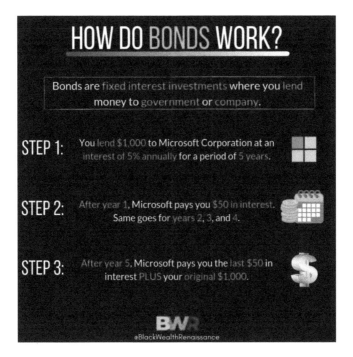

Bonds are a fixed income that is basically a loan to the borrower, which is usually a company or government. It can be looked at as an I.O.U. With interest for the lender and borrower. All levels of government & corporations use bonds to borrow money. The government needs bonds to build infrastructures such as roads and schools. When corporations need to raise capital to finance new projects, refinance debts, or maintain operations, they may issue bonds directly to investors. The borrower issues a bond that will include the terms of the loan, such as interest, repayments, and the time at which the loan, i.e., the bond principal, must be paid back, which is called the maturity date. The interest payment or the coupon is the return that the bondholders earn for loaning their funds to the borrower. The interest rate that determines the payment is called the coupon rate. The initial price of most bonds is typically centered around the face value per individual bond. Meaning, if the issuer issues a bond at $1,000, the face value is $1,000 initially. Due to fluctuating interest rates, once the bond is purchased initially, the price of the bond will fluctuate, depending on different market interest rates, while the face value (original value) will remain the same.

The initial bondholder can sell most bonds to other investors after the bond has been issued. In other words, a bond investor does not have to hold a bond all the way through to its maturity date. The actual market price of a bond depends on several factors: the length of the maturity date, the credit quality of the issuer, and the coupon rate compared to the general interest rate environment at the time. The face value of the bond is what will be paid back to the borrower once the bond matures. Meaning until the maturity date, you will be receiving interest payments, but once the maturity date comes, the issuer will pay you the face value of the bond.

Let's say Black Wealth Renaissance wants to build a new building for entrepreneurs to host their businesses & events. To fund this project, BWR issues bonds with a face value of $1,000 with a maturity date of 10 years, and to make it more attractive to investors; we decided to pay an interest rate of 5%. An investor will buy the bond at face value at $1,000, and they will be paid $50 a year for 10 years. On the bonds maturity date, the investor will redeem the bond and BWR will return his initial investment of $1,000. So in this example, the investor will have made $50 a year for ten years, which equals $500 and be given back his initial investment of $1,000, totaling a return on investment of $500. This is how bonds work and how they are a low-risk investment due to the bond being backed by the promise from the issuer.

ETFs

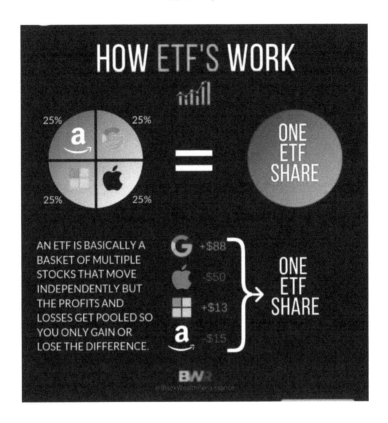

ETFs are short for exchange-traded funds; they are traded on the stock market like individual stocks. We would discuss individual stocks later on in this chapter. ETFs, pull money from investors together into a pool of different investments including stocks and bonds. An ETF can own hundreds or thousands of stocks across various industries, or it could be isolated to one particular industry or sector. With the ETF putting investments into multiple different **securities**[27] (stocks & bonds), it allows diversity creating less risk than investing in each stock or bond individually. Some ETFs simply mimic the stock market as a whole like the Vanguard S&P 500 ETF (VOO). VOO is the trading symbol for that Vanguard ETF.

Not only is there ETFs that mimic the total stock market but some ETFs mirror specific sectors of the stock market. For example, have you ever wanted to own stock in Apple, Microsoft, Google, and Facebook? Well, you can, for a pretty low cost. The ETF (IYW) shares U.S. Technology ETF has holdings in all these stocks and a lot more for around $220 during the writing of this ebook. When you purchase one share of (IYW), you will now own partial shares of each of those stocks, which creates your diversity in the stock market. Let's say Apple stock dropped $10 which is a dramatic loss for a stock, if you own the ETF (IYW) it will not drop a full $10 because it consists of more tech stocks that offset the loss of Apple.

Now let's discuss how do you make money holding ETFs in your investment portfolio. How you make money from an ETF will depend on the underlying investments of that ETF over time. Let's say you invest in the ETF SSGA US Large Cap Low Volatile ETF, which trades on the stock market with the ticker (SPDR). This ETF has holdings of Berkshire Hathaway Inc. B, Aflac Inc, Allstate Corp, and others. Let's say you bought 3 shares of this ETF in November of 2018 when it was trading at the price of $269. In November of 2019, the ETF traded at $311; you would have made a total of $126 in one year and a return of 15%, which is a great return in the stock market. So if you are interested in investing in ETFs, find a brokerage like Fidelity, TD

Ameritrade, Charles Schwabe, open an account and begin your journey.

MEDIUM RISK INVESTMENTS

MICRO INVESTING

When talking to individuals about investing in the stock market, one of the main things we always hear is, "I don't have enough money to invest in the stock market." To which our typical response is, "do you know what stock you want to invest in? And have you checked the price recently?" The chances are that most folks haven't. So, when we tell them that the power of smartphones allows us to invest in stocks at fractions of the price from the palm of our hands, they look at us like we are crazy. Some of you are probably looking at the device in your hands like it's crazy right now. It's not, and you're not, let us put you on game real quick. We want to introduce you to the wonders of micro-investing. Micro-investing is basically what the name entails which is investing micro amounts. Many individuals believe that you need large sums of money just to get started investing and that is simply not true. With micro-investing technology, your dollar can access **asset**[4] classes previously out of reach. For example, there's an app called M1 Finance that is our personal favorite to invest with. We like M1 because it's made for investors that have fractional amounts to invest. To open an account with M1 finance, you can go to their website at M1finance.com, or you download the app. From there, you can follow the prompts to set up your account and link your banking information. Once you've confirmed your account and funded it (minimum $100.00 and then $10.00 going forward). Up to this point, everything about M1 has been standard, but now is when things change, and they specialize.

So, M1 Finance is different from a lot of its competitors because of the ability to create your own ETFs called "pies." So, for example, let's say you were a car fanatic and wanted to invest in car companies. You could create a "pie" dedicated to companies you would like to invest in. So let's say the companies you particularly favor are Ford, Ferrari, Toyota, and Honda, and your birthday is in a couple of weeks. Now on your birthday, you're expecting some birthday money to go along with it and would like to stash some in your car pie containing your favorite companies. With M1 Finance, you can now put let's say $20 (assuming you've funded your account with the initial $100) in your account and have $5 applied to each section of your pie buying basically $5 worth of stock! Now, these shares won't provide huge returns most times but by being able to create your ETF and funded it with any amount you choose. You're taking a lot more power, and opportunity into the palm of your hands with M1 added to your portfolio.

Download M1 Finance at the link below

https://mbsy.co/CFBsn

PEER TO PEER LENDING

Prosper is just our personal choice when it comes to the micro-investing market that is peer to peer lending. Peer to peer lending with Prosper or Lending Club can allow you to micro invest starting at $25 and use your money like the bank! Peer to peer lending gives the average person the ability to loan their money to others in exchange for interest-bearing monthly payments, allowing their money to work for them just like a bank. Setting up your lending system is made very easy and straightforward by prosper. They have set up the onboarding process with two sides, lending, which is what we will primarily be focusing on, and their borrowing side where you can apply for loans. Our first steps will be signing up for your preferred peer to peer platform via their website and then linking your funding with your new account. Prosper allows you to get started with as little as $25 when funding the loans of your choice.

When choosing loans, you will have a plethora of options available to you. You will want to be strategic and diversified when building your portfolio of loan notes by thoroughly checking out who you're investing in and doing your due diligence before loaning your money. With that said, Jared has personally been investing with Prosper for about 2 years now, and he's only had one individual run late on loan. That person paid up their penalty fees, and he's been lucky enough to say that he hasn't had a loan default on me yet. *knocks on wood* Peer to peer lending can be a great way to grow your money based on your own risk tolerance because of the ability to choose who you are lending your money too and the very detailed credit profiles that you are provided. You decide your risk level and your interest rate, all while being the bank starting at $25, can't beat that.

EQUITY CROWDFUNDING

All businesses need capital to start, grow, and to have their impact on the world. Recently in the past year, Wordplay acquired FIS for 35 billion & SalesForce just recently bought Tableau for 15.7 billion. Now I know you are wondering what does that have to do with anything in this ebook. But let me explain as these companies that are getting bought out & acquired by bigger companies were not always this big. Most companies have to start from the grassroots, meaning they have to start small, build, & expand. When these companies are small & unknown, it is sometimes hard for the banks to loan them money. So they seek out for investors to help them bring in capital to work on projects, as well as grow their business.

In the past, it was almost impossible for the average person to invest in these companies, having to have been an accredited **investor**[2] to participate in these funding rounds. That all changed in 2012 with the passage of the Jumpstart Our Businesses (JOBS) Act, which allowed non accredited investors aka everyday people, to participate in early round investing in startup companies.

With the help of the internet, companies have found a new way to source the money they need from hundreds to thousands of investors called the "crowd." When crowdfunding first started, the crowd would invest in a business, project, or even an idea and would see a reward for their contribution. For example, I may come across a filmmaker on gofundme.com and want to help contribute to an upcoming film. In return, the filmmaker may give out tickets to their first viewing to those who contributed to the gofundme project. Now that you know how crowdfunding works let's discuss how you can make money with equity-based crowdfunding.

Investors have taken this idea of crowdfunding and have now come up with a way for investors to have a stake or share in the business they invest in. So, for example, let's say Black Wealth Renaissance is on an equity crowdfunding platform, and we are looking for $500,000 from investors in exchange for a 30% share of the company. Meaning Black Wealth Renaissance is looking for hundreds or even thousands of investors to contribute $500,000 for a total of 30% **equity**[15] in the company. You as an investor can invest as little as $1,000 into this crowdfund. Let's say you invest $7,500 in the crowdfund; you will have a 1.5% stake (ownership) in the 30% equity Black Wealth Renaissance is offering. It doesn't seem like much, but let's say Black Wealth Renaissance did $250,000 in profit for 3 years straight. You would receive $1,125 for three straight years, with an **ROI**[25] of 15%. To go further into equity crowdfunding, let's say Black Wealth Renaissance was bought out by our friends at

Blacker Pockets for $800,000, you would receive $3,600.

Now that we have discussed the good equity crowdfunding, it does come with risk. In the previous example, if the Black Wealth Renaissance were to lose $150,000 for three straight years, the opposite would be true. You would have lost all of your investment & would have a negative ROI. This is just something you need to understand before you invest in equity crowdfunding. There are many different equity crowdfunding platforms such as Angelist, CircleUp, and Fundable just to name a few.

HIGH-RISK INVESTMENTS

FOREX

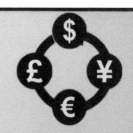

WHAT IS FOREX????

- Formally known as the foriegn exchange market it is the largest and most liquid trading market in the world
- In this market currencies are bought and sold against each other in pairs (ex: EUR-USD)
- The market is not centralized and trades are executed in an over the counter fashion on various platforms
- Trading occurs 24 hrs a day 5 days a week and can be done from your phone, tablet, and/or computer

Have you ever traveled to a foreign country and needed to exchange your U.S. currency into the currency of the country you are traveling to? In essence, this is exactly what Forex trading is, Forex is short for Foreign Exchange. Corporations need to purchase products from other countries, and before they can do so, they must convert their native currency into the currency in which they are purchasing the goods. The difference between corporations & people exchanging currency is that companies do this in huge amounts. When these corporations exchange these huge amounts, they will actually increase the worth of the currency due to the demand for the increasing currency. As demand increases, the price increases.

So when currencies are exchanged they are exchanged at a certain price, called the exchange rate. Due to currency exchanges happening across the globe almost non stop, the exchange rates are constantly changing. Like most markets, the currency price is determined by supply & demand. If many people want to change dollars into euros, the price of the euro will rise against the dollar. This causes the exchange rate to shift in favor of the euro.

Let's look at an example and how you can make money from exchanging currencies. Let's say you went on a summer vacation to Europe from the United States. Let's say you changed your $500 into euros at the rate of 1.40 euros for every dollar, giving you 700 euros. While on this vacation you didn't spend any of the 700 euros, so you travel back to the U.S. with 700 euros. Since you are back in the country, you need to convert the euros back into U.S. dollars. During the currency exchange process, you notice that the exchange rate has changed from 1.4 to 1.3 euros for every dollar. Instead of just getting 500 dollars back, you received $538 back. Allowing you to make a $38 profit just from exchanging currencies. This is exactly how the Forex market works and how people make thousands in this realm. Investors buy a certain amount of a currency, hold on to it while the exchange rates change, and then exchange it back for a profit. There are many different strategies and ways to make money in the Forex market; please make sure you do your due diligence before investing in it.

INDIVIDUAL STOCKS

When people think of investing a lot of time, you will think of investing in the stock market. This can seem like a very risky, slightly scary way to invest, especially if you don't understand how the stock market works. So let's break it down, let's say you have built a business and want to expand. You will need the capital to do so, to gain the capital necessary, you decided to break down your company into "shares" (a percentage of ownership in the company). You decide to sell each share to investors. Before you start selling shares, you still made sure you owned a majority of the shares, so that you were in control of the business. This is a simple example of the basics of the stock market. People buy & sell shares of companies to seek profit or equity in corporations. This process of opening the public to buy shares of your company is called an initial public offering (IPO).

Facebook is the biggest leader in the social media industry. If we take a look at Mark Zuckerburg (the founder of Facebook), we can see how he raised over 16 billion dollars through the stock market. Facebook went public in 2012, with 337 million shares with a price of $38 per share. Meaning back in 2012, you could've own part of Facebook for as little as $38. When Mark realized that people were buying too many shares, he noticed he had too much demand, not enough supply. So, he added 84 million shares bringing Facebook to a total of 421 million shares. Facebook sold every single share, all 421 million shares making Mark Zuckerburg & Facebook a billion dollars in just hours.

Now that you've seen the benefit of the company's going public and offering shares of their company, you are probably wondering how you can make money investing in these companies through the stock market. Going back to Facebook, on the same day as the IPO, the stock price rose from $38 a share to $45 a share. So let's say back in 2012, you bought $500 worth of the Facebook IPO while it was $38 a share. You would have bought 13 shares of Facebook (FB is the trading symbol on the stock market). The stock rose to $45, meaning you would have made $7 on each share that you own. Since you own 13 shares, you would have made $91 in just hours, and this $91 increase is called capital gains. You should also remember that there are tax implications with capital gains such as if you hold a stock for a year or less you will be taxed at your current income tax rate. If you were to hold a stock for longer than a year you will be taxed at the long term capital gains rate which is 15%. This is just something to keep in mind if you are thinking about investing in the stock market.

Another way to make money in stocks is through dividends. A dividend is money paid from the company to investors who hold shares of the company. To further understand dividends, let's again go back to our Facebook example. Theoretically, when you buy a stock, you become the owner of the company. This means you and other investors who buy the company's stock have the right to receive some of the profits from the company. When you purchased 10 shares of Facebook back in 2012, you are now an owner of Facebook like billionaire Mark Zuckerburg. So let's say Facebook makes 15.9 Billion dollars, how much of the net income do you receive? You purchased 13 shares when in total, there were 421 million shares available. It sounds like your shares aren't worth much, but let's continue to take a deeper dive into this example. If we divide the net income (15.9 billion) by the total number of shares (421 million) it equals 37.77. This is called earnings per share (EPS); this means each stock of Facebook should earn you $37.77. In other words, your 13 stocks are supposed to earn you $491.01. Again this is just hypothetically; Facebook will not send you a check for that amount.

The amount they will send is determined by a group of people called the board of directors. Board of directors, a lot of times, want shareholders to maintain their stake in the company, so they issue out dividends from their profits. You could look at it as a form of a thank you card from the company.

Some companies have a board of directors that make dividends their top priority, such as International Business Machines Corp, aka IBM. Now, this is not investment advice for you to invest in IBM; we are just acknowledging their efforts on continuously paying high dividend yields. The dividend yield is basically the ROI (return on investment) of the dividend based on the price of the stock. So let's say IBM has a stock price of $134, and they issue out dividend of $6 per share annually the dividend yield would be 4.48% (which is pretty good). Also, meaning if you owned 10 shares of IBM, you would be paid $60 just from owning its stock. This is how people make millions in the stock market. To get started investing in the stock market, you need first to find a brokerage that works for you, and many offer 0% commission fees, which will be putting more money in your pocket.

A QUICK OVERVIEW OF INVESTING IN STOCKS THAT PAY DIVIDENDS.

BW
@BlackWealthRennaisance

Example: NYMT

Price = $6.15

Dividend = $0.20

$5,000 investment

813 shares x $0.20 = $162 per quarter

$162 per quarter averages to $54 per month

Use this to pay your phone bill

BUY ASSETS TO PAY FOR LIABILITIES

REAL ESTATE

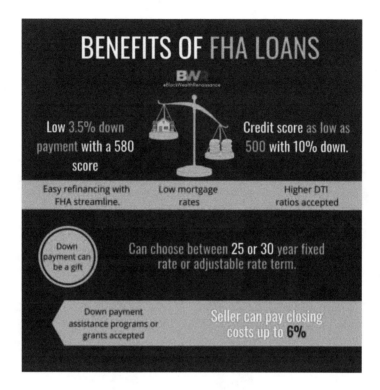

The real estate industry is where a lot of the 1% make their money. It's one of the best ways to increase your net worth from 0 to six figures. Looking into real estate investing can make you very hesitant especially looking at the amount you may have to invest. We are going to dive into three ways that you can invest in real estate without having an enormous amount of cash.

The Federal Housing Administration (FHA) loan is becoming increasingly popular for first time home buyers. It requires a low down payment of 3.5% for people with a credit score of 580 and above. Meaning with an FHA loan, you can get a loan for up to 96.5% of the value of the property. Which is a great way to leverage your money and not have to pay 10-15% down payment for a conventional loan. An FHA loan is quite friendly. It's almost impossible to get approved for a conventional mortgage with a credit score below 620. It's imperative to note that the lower the credit score, the higher the interest rate; therefore, you need to make sure you have a decent credit score.

So how can you make money with an FHA loan, you may ask? With an FHA loan, you can pay a 3.5% down payment on a multi-unit property. The goal of using this loan to acquire such properties is to live in one unit and rent the other out which is called house hacking. House hacking is a way for you to live for "free" and possibly still make money from others paying you rent. The maximum number of units you can purchase with an FHA loan is 4 units at the max value of $605,525. For example, let's say You buy a triplex (3 unit property) for $180,000 with an FHA loan. You would have to put a down payment of $6,300 for the property & also pay 1.5% of the mortgage insurance premium of $180,000. That adds up to around $9,450 to acquire this property plus closing cost & realtor fees. With this FHA loan, your monthly payment, including the loan principal, interest, insurance, and taxes, would be around $1,240. Going with the house hacking route, you will live in one unit and rent out the other two units for $700 a month. This means you would receive $1,400 in rent from two tenants covering your $1,240 expenses and have a profit of 160 dollars a month. This allows you not only to live rent-free but you also just gave yourself an extra $1,920 a year in income from being creative with your FHA loan.

I know some of you are reading this and wondering what if I have already purchased a home? Well, here's a way to leverage the home you already have into a rental property. Equity in a house is considered to be the difference in what the home is worth & what you owe on the home. Equity in a home can come from a multitude of things. You can gain equity in a home from value going up on your house or the houses around you. You can also gain equity in your home just by paying down the amount you owe on your home. For example, let's say you own a home with a value of $200,000, and you originally bought the house at $160,000. You now have $40,000 in equity in the home. In that same example, you also have paid half of the original $160,000 loan. You would now have $120,000 worth of equity in the home, $40,000 from the value of the home going up (appreciation), and $80,000 from paying off the loan. With this $120,000, you can take out a loan (a 2nd mortgage) on the house called Home Equity Line of Credit (HELOC). It is similar to getting access to a credit card with a total credit of up to 90% of the home value (180,000 in this example).

I know some of you are thinking that the interest rate has to be ridiculous, but in most cases, the interest rate on a **HELOC**[17] is lower than credit cards sometimes can be as low as 5%. So if our mortgage is $80,000 and the bank will allow us to take out $180,000, we will have $100,000 that we can pull out for a home equity line of credit. That means now you can use this $100,000 to purchase real estate. Let's say you are buying a rental property for $80,000; you still have $20,000 for incidentals, repairs, and taxes. With this newly acquired rental property, you charge $750 for rent. Meaning you will now bring in $9,000 a year just from rental income. HELOCs are a great strategy to use if you have a lot of equity in your home.

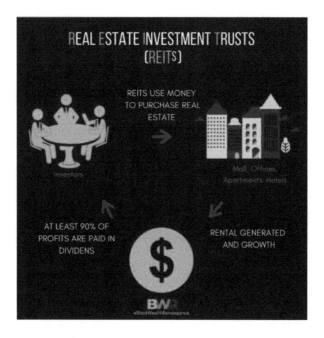

Another way to invest in real estate for a minimal amount is REITs (Real Estate Investment Trust). REITs were created to allow people to invest in income-producing real estate. REITs allow anyone to own or finance properties with minimum cost. REITs can be traded on the stock market, just like individual stocks. Similar to how shareholders receive a dividend for owning a stock, shareholders of a REIT earn a share of the profit produced from the real estate it invested in. Meaning you will earn money from just holding a share of the REIT without having to buy, finance, or repair properties. There are two types of REITS, equity and mortgage REITs. Equity REITs own a variety of properties from office buildings, shopping centers, and even hotels. Equity REITs receive most of their revenue from rent on those properties, but Mortgage REITs may have residential or commercial properties in its portfolio. Mortgage REITs get most of their revenue from the interest on mortgages or mortgage-backed securities. What makes REITs so investor-friendly is that they are required to distribute 90% of their taxable income to their shareholders as dividends. Some REITs pay out their dividends monthly such as American Capital Agency Corporation (AGNC). As of November 2019, they had a dividend yield of 11.53% at $1.92 per share and were traded at $17.32. Meaning you can start owning a portfolio of real estate that pays you monthly for only $17. REITs are a great way to receive dividends on commercial or

residential real estate for minimum cost.

COMMON MISTAKES NEW INVESTORS MAKE

1) OVERLEVERAGING
IMPROPER MANGEMENT OF RISK CAUSES GREATER LOSSES AND LEADS TO POOR PERFORMANCE

2) CHASING TRENDS
IF EVERYONE IS TALKING ABOUT IT THE REAL MONEY HAS ALREADY BEEN MADE I.E. BITCOIN

3) THINKING TOO SHORT TERM
MANY HOP INTO THE MARKET THINKING THAT THEY WILL GAIN RICHES AND SEE MASSIVE SUCCESS OVERNIGHT

4) NOT KNOWING WHEN TO CUT THEIR LOSSES
HOLDING AN INVESTMENT AFTER IT TAKES A NEGATIVE TURN IN THE HOPES THAT IT WILL SWING BACK UP IS A GREAT WAY TO LOSE MONEY

5) LACK OF MARKET RESEARCH
GROWING POPULARITY AND LOWER BARRIERS OF ENTRY HAVE PEOPLE HOPPING INTO MARKETS WITHOUT UNDERSTANDING HOW THEY OPERATE

@BLACKWEALTHRENAISSANC

<u>CONCLUSION</u>

In short, we're not here to tell you the right or wrong way to build wealth because the answer depends on too many factors. Your personal risk tolerance, goals, and avenues you choose to use to invest will determine how your journey to financial independence will look. A risky individual with a lot of money may have a completely different journey than someone with lower risk tolerance, and that's completely okay.

So now comes the next steps. Planning, preparation, and action! This isn't one of those feel-good "ahhh I learned so much, and now I'm just gonna sit on it" books. I want you to take action! I want you to download a budget, our budget! Get on blackwealthrenaissance.com right now and stop your bleeding. Research ways to boost your income and find ways you feel comfortable with putting your money to work for you today. You work too hard to have your money not working just as hard for you. But, we do want you to understand that this is just the beginning; this journey will not be easy, and will probably not be quick. But it will definitely be worth it. We at Black Wealth Renaissance believe financial independence is truly achievable for any individual, and we hope that we have given you some helpful tools to start your journey at least. Remember, the best time to get started investing was 20 years ago; the second-best time is today!

GLOSSARY

1. **401k -** is a tax-advantaged, defined-contribution retirement account offered by many employers to their employees.

2. **Accredited Investor -**

3. **Appreciation -** an increase in the value of an asset over time.

4. **Asset** - Puts Money Into Your Pocket

5. **APR -** annual percentage rate (APR) is the annual rate charged for borrowing or earned through an investment.

6. **Avalanche Method -** a debtor allocates enough money to make the minimum payment on each source of debt, then devotes any remaining repayment funds to the debt with the highest interest rate

7. **Bad Debt -** if you are borrowing money to purchase depreciating assets. Ex. Cars, Consumer Electronics, etc.

8. **Balance Transfers** - used by consumers who want to move the amount they owe to a credit card with a lower interest rate, fewer penalties, and better benefits such as rewards points or travel miles.

9. **Brokerage Account-** A bank account for investing

10. **Cashflow** - Cash flow is the net amount of cash and cash-equivalents being transferred into and out of a business.

11. **Debt Consolidation** - Multiple debts are combined into a single, larger piece of debt, usually with more favorable payoff terms.

12. **Dividends** - share of a company's profits passed on to the shareholders (stock owner) periodically.

13. **Due Diligence-** Means to do personal research on the matter

14. **Emergency fund** - a readily available reserve of cash/assets to help one

navigate financial dilemmas such as the loss of a job, a debilitating illness, or a major repair to your home or car.

15. **Equity** - Equity is typically referred to as shareholder equity, which represents the amount of money that would be returned to a company's shareholders if all of the assets were liquidated and all of the company's debt was paid off.

16. **Good Debt** - Good debt is exemplified in the old adage "it takes money to make money." If the debt you take on helps you to generate income and increase your net worth, that can be considered positive

17. **HELOC** - Home equity lines of credit are like a revolving source of funds, much like a credit card, that you use as you see fit.

18. **Individual Retirement Account (IRA)** - a tax-advantaged investing tool that

individuals use to earmark funds for retirement savings

19. **Interest Rates** - The interest rate is the amount a lender charges for the use of assets expressed as a percentage of the principal

20. **IPO** - Initial Public Offering is when companies sell their stock for the first time to the public.

21. **Liability**- Takes money out your pocket.

22. **Maturity Date** - The maturity date is the date on which the principal amount of a note, draft, acceptance bond or other debt instrument becomes due

23. **Personal Budget** - A budget is an estimation of income and expenses over a specified period of time and is usually re-evaluated on a periodic basis.

24. **Risk Tolerance** - To keep it simple be defined as how much money are you

comfortable taking a loss on within an investment.

25. **ROI** - Return on Investment (ROI) is a performance measure used to evaluate the efficiency of an investment or to compare the efficiency of a number of different investments.

26. **Roth Ira** - A Roth IRA is a tax-advantaged, retirement savings account that allows you to withdraw your savings tax-free.

27. **Securities** - tradable financial assets, such as equities or fixed income instruments EX-stock, money, bonds

28. **Self Education** - this is the integral process that you are practicing right now by reading this book. Self education is the most important education because it makes up for what traditional education lacks.

29. **Share** - Ownership of a full stock in a company.

30. **Snowball method** - a method of debt repayment in which the debtor lists each of his/her debts from smallest to largest

31. **Stock** - A piece of ownership in a company

32. **Stock Options** - A stock option gives an investor the right, but not the obligation, to buy or sell a stock at an agreed upon price and date. There are two types of options: puts, which is a bet that a stock will fall, or calls, which is a bet that a stock will rise.

33. **Taxable Account** - Any account that can be taxed, EX- Banks, Investments, Retirement.

RESOURCES

TrueBill   -
https://apps.apple.com/us/app/truebill-budget-
bill-tracker/id1130616675

HOW TO MANAGE YOUR MONEY LIKE THE 1%

CPSIA information can be obtained
at www.ICGtesting.com
Printed in the USA
LVHW052346100720
660358LV00008B/443